English Made Super Easy 2
英语超级容易学2

JOSCELYN QUEK

PARTRIDGE

To order additional copies of this book, contact
Toll Free 800 101 2657 (Singapore)
Toll Free 1 800 81 7340 (Malaysia)
orders.singapore@partridgepublishing.com

www.partridgepublishing.com/singapore

目录

1. 不同类型的句子

Different types of Sentences

Above 之上

1. We looked at the stars above us.
   我们看着天上的星星。

2. He hang the picture above the sofa.
   他把照片挂在沙发上。

3. He pointed at the ceiling above us.
   他指着我们头顶上的天花板。

4. His result is above my expectation.
   他的成绩出乎我的意料。。

5. The fan is above the dining table.
   风扇在餐桌上方。

6. We enjoy watching the clouds above us.
   我们喜欢看天上的云。

7. The baby looked at the camera above him.
   婴儿看着他上面的相机。

8. The interest rate is above five percent.
   利息是五巴仙以上。

Below 之下

1. We sat below the tree.
   我们坐在树下。

2. We rested below the coconut tree.
   我们在椰树下休息。

3. We hid below the table.
   我们躲在桌子下面了。

4. The pail is below the fan.
   桶在风扇的下面。

5. The ball is below the bed.
   球在床的下面。

6. He lay below his car.
   他躺在他的车下面。

7. The puppy slept below the sofa.
   小狗睡在沙发下面。

8. The rat hid below the piano.
   老鼠躲在钢琴下面。

Along 沿

1. We walked along the beach.
   我们沿着海滩漫步。

2. We cycled along the road.
   我们沿着这条路骑车。

3. We jogged along the river.
   我们沿着河慢跑。

4. We marched along the road.
   我们沿着这条路行进。

5. We strolled along the pond.
   我们沿着池塘散步。

6. We lined up along the fence.
   我们沿着篱笆排队。

7. We queued up along the pavement.
   我们沿着人行道排队。

8. We walked along the lake.
   我们沿着湖边漫步。

Through   通过

1. We walked through the tunnel.
我们穿过了隧道。

2. We walked through the market.
我们走过了市场。

3. We walked through the jungle.
我们穿过丛林。

4. We walked through the underpass.
我们穿过地道。

5. He came in through the window.
他从窗户进来了。

6. He looked through a microscope.
他透过显微镜观察。

7. He glanced through the magazine.
他翻阅了杂志。

8. We breath through our nose.
我们通过我们的鼻子呼吸。

Gerunds　动名词

1. They went shopping.
   他们去购物。

2. They like fishing.
   他们喜欢钓鱼。

3. She went jogging in the morning.
   她早上去跑步。

4. She likes watching TV.
   她喜欢看电视。

5. They love dancing.
   他们喜欢跳舞。

6. She likes traveling.
   她喜欢旅行。

7. They enjoy cycling.
   他们喜欢骑自行车。

8. She is very good at drawing.
   她很会画画。

Adverbs 副词

1. They sang happily.
   他们开心地唱歌。

2. She cried sadly.
   她伤心地哭了。

3. They donated generously to the orphanage.
   他们慷慨地捐赠给孤儿院。

4. She shouted loudly.
   她大声地喊。

5. She speaks confidently.
   她自信地说。

6. They slept soundly.
   他们睡得很香。

7. They walked in quietly.
   他们悄悄地走进。

8. She worked diligently.
   她勤奋工作。

Always 总是

1. He is always late.
他总是迟到。

2. You are always punctual.
你总是守时。

3. You always bully her.
你总是欺负她。

4. He always borrows money from me.
他总是向我借钱。

5. He always makes mistakes.
他总是犯错。

6. You are always very playful.
你总是很调皮。

7. He always donates generously.
他总是慷慨捐赠。

8. He is always aggressive.
他总是气势汹汹。

Often 常常

1. She often helps her neighbours.
她常常帮她的邻居们。

2. She often goes skiing.
她常常去滑雪。

3. She often lends money to her friends.
她常常借钱给朋友。

4. She often loses her credit cards.
她常常遗失她的信用卡。

5. They often visit the orphanage.
他们常常探访这间孤儿院。

6. They often attend birthday parties.
他们常常参加生日会。

7. She often falls sick.
她常常生病。

8. They often go to Europe.
他们常常去欧洲。

Seldom   很少

1. We seldom go to the post office.
   我们很少去邮政局。

2. She seldom talks to me.
   她很少跟我讲话。

3. We seldom play computer games.
   我们很少玩电脑游戏。

4. She seldom quarrels with her husband.
   她很少跟她的丈夫吵架。

5. We seldom go to the jungle.
   我们很少去丛林。

6. She seldom buys branded bags.
   她很少买名牌皮包。

7. We seldom eat Italian food.
   我们很少吃意大利餐。

8. She seldom borrows money from me.
   她很少向我借钱。

Usually 通常

1. He usually wakes up late.
   他通常醒晚。

2. He usually eats supper.
   他通常吃宵夜。

3. We usually go fishing on Saturday.
   我们通常星期六去钓鱼。

4. We usually walk home.
   我们通常步行回家。

5. He usually listens to pop songs.
   他通常听流行歌曲。

6. He usually buys his grocery at the supermarket.
   他通常在超市买他的杂货。

7. We usually drive to work.
   我们通常开车去上班。

8. We usually take our lunch at 1 pm.
   我们通常在1点吃午饭。

Never 从来没有

1. I have never met her.
   我从来没有见过她。

2. I have never visited my uncle.
   我从来没有拜访过我的叔叔。

3. I have never praised my daughter.
   我从来没有称赞过我的女儿。

4. I have never tasted durians.
   我从来没有吃过榴莲。

5. I have never learnt swimming.
   我从来没有学过游泳。

6. I have never argued with him.
   我从来没有和他争论过。

7. He has never learnt skiing.
   他从来没有学过滑雪。

8. He has never tasted pizza.
   他从来没有吃过披萨。

And 和

1. She is tall and thin.
她又高又瘦。

2. They are rich and famous.
他们是富有和著名的。

3. She lost her way and cried loudly.
她迷路了, 哭得很大声。

4. They were very frightened and called the police.
他们非常害怕, 并报警了。

5. She was a nurse and worked in Raffles Hospital.
她是一名护士, 在莱佛士医院工作。

6. They were intelligent and hardworking.
他们聪明又勤劳。

7. She is gentle and sweet.
她温柔又甜美。

8. They lead and encourage the students.
他们领导和鼓励学生们。

Once 一次

1. Once, I went to his shop.
   有一次，我去他的店。

2. Once, I complained to the principal.
   有一次，我向校长投诉。

3. Once, I asked him to help me.
   有一次，我叫他帮忙我。

4. Once, she failed her English test.
   有一次，她的英文测验不及格。

5. Once, she bought a very expensive dress.
   有一次，她买了一件很贵的连衣裙。

6. Once, I lost my wallet.
   有一次， 我丢了钱包。

7. Once, she stole my money.
   有一次，她偷了我的钱。

8. Once, her father fainted on the street.
   有一次，她父亲在街上晕倒了。

Also 也

1. He also speaks Spanish.
   他也会说西班牙语。

2. They also like to drink coffee.
   他们也喜欢喝咖啡。

3. He also works very hard.
   他也很努力地工作。

4. They are also very talented.
   他们也很有才华。

5. He is also very humorous.
   他也很幽默。

6. He also donated a lot of money.
   他还捐了很多钱。

7. They also love music.
   他们也喜欢音乐。

8. He also signed up for the course.
   他也报读了这个课程。

Still 仍然

1. They are still very childish.
   他们仍然很幼稚。

2. They are still very busy.
   他们仍然很忙。

3. She is still very helpful.
   她仍然很乐意帮助人。

4. It is still very cold.
   天气仍然很冷。

5. She still looks very pale.
   她看起来仍然很苍白。

6. They are still very stubborn.
   他们仍然很固执。

7. They are still very optimistic.
   他们仍然很乐观。

8. She is still very energetic.
   她仍然精力充沛。

Consequently　因此

1. Consequently, his boss fired him.
   因此，他的老板解雇了他。

2. Consequently, he missed his flight.
   因此，他错过了他的班机。

3. Consequently, he lost his passport.
   因此，他失去了他的护照。

4. Consequently, his teacher scolded him.
   因此，他的老师骂他。

5. Consequently, he lost his way.
   因此，他迷路了。

6. Consequently, he became very ill.
   因此，他病倒了。

7. Consequently, he went to jail.
   因此，他进了监狱。

8. Consequently, he became very famous.
   因此，他变得非常出名。

However   然而

1. However, he still loves us.
   然而，他仍然爱我们。

2. However, he is very caring.
   然而，他很有爱心。

3. However, we forgive him.
   然而，我们原谅他。

4. However, he has been very supportive.
   然而，他一直很支持我们。

5. However, he did not blame us.
   然而，他没有责怪我们。

6. However, we still enjoy gardening.
   然而，我们仍然喜欢园艺。

7. However, we managed to arrive on time.
   然而，我们设法准时到达了。

8. However, he agreed to support us.
   然而，他同意支持我们了。

Furthermore   此外

1. Furthermore, he owes the bank a lot of money.
   此外，他欠银行很多钱。

2. Furthermore, he gave me a bouquet of flowers.
   此外，他给了我一束花。

3. Furthermore, they are successful businessmen.
   此外，他们是成功的商人。

4. Furthermore, they come to help us every week.
   此外，他们每周都来帮助我们。

5. Furthermore, he has earned a lot of money.
   此外，他赚了很多钱。

6. Furthermore, he is a filial son.
   此外，他是一个孝顺的儿子。

7. Furthermore, he is very creative.
   此外，他很有创意。

8. Furthermore, they are very experienced.
   此外，他们很有经验。

Nevertheless　尽管如此

1. Nevertheless, she continued to play with us.
尽管如此，她继续和我们一起玩。

2. Nevertheless, no one was hurt.
尽管如此，没有人受伤。

3. Nevertheless, they did not ask us to leave.
尽管如此，他们没有要求我们离开。

4. Nevertheless, they arrived safely.
尽管如此，他们安全到达了。

5. Nevertheless, she did not complain to the principal.
尽管如此，她没有向校长投诉。

6. Nevertheless, she still looks young.
尽管如此，她看起来还年轻。

7. Nevertheless, they agreed to help us.
尽管如此，他们同意帮助我们。

8. Nevertheless, they had a great day.
尽管如此，他们度过了美好的一天。

Myself   自己

1. I do it myself.
   我自己做。

2. I go to the market myself.
   我自己去菜市场。

3. I chose the clothes myself.
   我自己选了这些衣服。

4. I wrote the essay myself.
   我自己写这篇文章。

5. I decorated the house myself.
   我自己装饰房子。

6. I baked the muffins myself.
   我自己烘制这些松饼。

7. I selected the bracelet myself.
   我自己挑选这手镯。

8. I changed the light bulb myself.
   我自己换灯泡。

1. You do it yourself.
   你自己做。

2. You booked the air ticket yourself.
   你自己订了机票。

3. You wrote the song yourself.
   你自己写了这首歌。

4. You changed the tire yourself.
   你自己换了轮胎。

5. You went to the library yourself.
   你自己去了图书馆。

6. You painted the house yourself.
   你自己粉刷了房子。

7. You mailed the letter yourself.
   你自己寄了信。

8. You purchased the air conditioner
   yourself.
   你自己购买了空调。

1. We do it ourselves.
   我们自己做。

2. We renovated the house ourselves.
   我们自己翻新了屋子。

3. We drew the flowers ourselves.
   我们自己画了花。

4. We bought the furniture ourselves.
   我们自己买了家具。

5. We went camping ourselves.
   我们自己去露营。

6. We baked the cookies ourselves.
   我们自己烘饼干。

7. We planned the wedding ourselves.
   我们自己筹备婚礼。

8. We did the makeup ourselves.
   我们自己化妆。

1. They do it themselves.
   他们自己做。

2. They built the house themselves.
   他们自己建房子。

3. They fried the chicken wings themselves.
   他们自己炸鸡翅。

4. They manufactured the toys themselves.
   他们自己制造玩具。

5. They decorated their restaurant
   themselves.
   他们自己装饰自己的餐馆。

6. They filled in the forms themselves.
   他们自己填写表格。

7. They delivered the goods themselves.
   他们自己送货。

8. They found out the truth themselves.
   他们自己查明真相。

1. He does it himself.
   他自己做。

2. He cleaned the toilet himself.
   他自己洗了厕所。

3. He called the police himself.
   他自己报警了。

4. He wrote the report himself.
   他自己写了报告。

5. He takes care of his children himself.
   他自己照顾孩子。

6. He cancelled the trip himself.
   他自己取消了旅行。

7. He wrote the resume himself.
   他自己写简历。

8. He flew to London himself.
   他亲自飞往伦敦。

1. She did it herself.
   她自己做的。

2. She coloured her hair herself.
   她自己染了头发。

3. She designed the wedding gown herself.
   她自己设计了婚纱礼服。

4. She wrote the poem herself.
   她自己写了这首诗歌。

5. She planned the itinerary herself.
   她自己计划了行程。

6. She organised the party herself.
   她自己举办了这个派对。

7. She revealed the secret herself.
   她自己揭露了这个秘密。

8. She took the photographs herself.
   她自己拍了这些照片。

Mine   我的

1. This watch is mine.
   这支手表是我的。

2. This rice cooker is mine.
   这个电饭煲是我的。

3. This document is mine.
   这份文件是我的。

4. This apartment is mine.
   这间公寓是我的。

5. These utensils are mine.
   这些器皿是我的。

6. These envelopes are mine.
   这些信封是我的。

7. This identity card is mine.
   这张身份证是我的。

8. These trophies are mine.
   这些奖杯是我的。

1. That oven is yours.
   那个烤箱是你的。

2. Those letters are yours.
   那些信是你的。

3. That sport car is yours.
   那辆跑车是你的。

4. Those sweet potatoes are yours.
   那些红薯是你的。

5. That guitar is yours.
   那把吉他是你的。

6. That apron is yours.
   那条围裙是你的。

7. Those sandals are yours.
   那些凉鞋是你的。

8. Those furnitures are yours.
   那些家具是你的。

1. This land is ours.
   这土地是我们的。

2. These dictionaries are ours.
   这些字典是我们的。

3. This vacuum cleaner is ours.
   这个吸尘机是我们的。

4. These bookshelves are ours.
   这些书架是我们的。

5. This shop is ours.
   这家商店是我们的。

6. These strawberries are ours.
   这些草莓是我们的。

7. This ironIng board is ours.
   这熨衣板是我们的。

8. These factories are ours.
   这些工厂是我们的。

1. That boat is theirs.
   那艘船是他们的。

2. That farm is theirs.
   那个农场是他们的。

3. That fridge is theirs.
   那个冰箱是他们的。

4. That hammer is theirs.
   那把锤子是他们的。

5. That horse is theirs.
   那匹马是他们的。

6. That building is theirs.
   那栋楼是他们的。

7. These houses are theirs.
   这些房子是他们的。

8. These documents are theirs.
   这些文件是他们的。

1. That apartment is his.
   那间公寓是他的。

2. That briefcase is his.
   那个公文包是他的。

3. That warehouse is his.
   那个仓库是他的。

4. That story book is his.
   那本故事书是他的。

5. That tea pot is his.
   那个茶壶是他的。

6. That mobile phone is his.
   那个手机是他的。

7. That massage chair is his.
   那张按摩椅是他的。

8. That van is his.
   那辆面包车是他的。

1. This necklace is hers.
   这条项链是她的。

2. This kettle is hers.
   这个水壶是她的。

3. That evening gown is hers.
   那件晚礼服是她的。

4. That hairpin is hers.
   那个发夹是她的。

5. This juicer is hers.
   这个榨汁机是她的。

6. That blender is hers.
   那个搅拌机是她的。

7. This scarf is hers.
   这条围巾是她的。

8. That wig is hers.
   那假发是她的。

Comparative of Adjectives
比较式形容词

1. She is shorter than me.
   她比我矮。

2. I am fatter than him.
   我比他胖。

3. David is older than John.
   大卫的年纪比约翰大。

4. I am taller than you.
   我比你高。

5. Jane is more cheerful than Mary.
   珍妮比玛丽开朗。

6. She is more intelligent than me.
   她比我聪明。

7. You are more talented than me.
   你比我更有才华。

8. I am more excited than him.
   我比他更兴奋。

Joscelyn Quek

Superlative of Adjectives
最高级形容词

1. He is the shortest student in his class.
   他在班上是最矮的学生。

2. She is the youngest member in the club.
   她是俱乐部里最年轻的会员。

3. Jane is the prettiest girl in her school.
   珍在学校是最漂亮的女孩。

4. Kenny is the tallest boy in the team.
   肯尼在队中是最高的男生。

5. Mr Yang is the richest man in the group.
   杨先生是集团里最富有的人。

6. He is the most stingy member in the club.
   他是俱乐部里最吝啬的成员。

7. He is the most hardworking employee in the company.
   他是公司里工作最勤奋的员工。

8. He is the most handsome model in Italy.
   他是意大利最英俊的模特儿。

Prefer   比较喜欢

1. I prefer grapes to bananas.
   我喜欢葡萄胜过香蕉。

2. I prefer coffee to tea.
   我喜欢咖啡多过茶。

3. I prefer to be alone.
   我比较喜欢独处。

4. prefer walking to jogging.
   我喜欢走路多过慢跑。

5. I prefer singing to dancing.
   我喜欢唱歌胜过跳舞。

6. She prefers roses to tulips.
   她喜欢玫瑰胜过郁金香。

7. He prefers jogging to fishing.
   他喜欢慢跑胜过钓鱼。

8. He prefers cakes to cookies.
   他喜欢蛋糕胜过饼干。

Either　或

1. Either Tom or Mary is playing the game now.
汤姆或玛丽现在在玩游戏。

2. Either Tom or Mary won the first prize.
汤姆或玛丽赢了头奖。

3. Either Tom or Mary went to America.
汤姆或玛丽去了美国。

4. Either Tom or Mary bought the roast duck.
汤姆或玛丽买了烤鸭。

5. Either Tom or Mary found the kitten.
不是汤姆就是玛丽找到了那只小猫。

6. Either Tom or Mary likes music.
汤姆或玛丽喜欢音乐。

7. Either Jack or Li Fen ironed the clothes.
杰克或丽芬熨烫了那些衣服。

8. Either Jack or Li Fen suffers from depression.
不是杰克就是丽芬患有抑郁症。

Neither　　两个都不

1. Neither Susan nor Mr. Lee likes the idea.
   苏珊和李先生都不喜欢这个想法。

2. Neither Susan nor Mr. Lee speaks French.
   苏珊和李先生都不会说法语。

3. Neither Susan nor Mr. Lee enjoys fishing.
   苏珊和李先生都不喜欢钓鱼。

4. Neither Susan nor Mr. Lee told the reporter.
   苏珊和李先生都没有告诉记者。

5. Neither Susan nor Mr. Lee likes to eat durians.
   苏珊和李先生都不喜欢吃榴莲。

6. Neither Susan nor Mr. Lee locked the door.
   苏珊和李先生都没有锁上门。

7. Neither she nor her husband disciplines their son.
   她和她的丈夫都不管教他们的儿子。

8. Neither Mr Li nor Mr Wang appreciates classical music.
   李先生和王先生都不欣赏古典音乐。

Passive Voice 被动词

1. He is punished by his teacher.
   他受到老师的惩罚。

2. I was scolded by my father last night.
   昨晚我被父亲骂了一顿。

3. Mary is trained by her mother.
   玛丽是由她的母亲训练的。

4. John was criticised by his colleagues last week.
   约翰上周被同事批评了。

5. I am consoled by my friends.
   我被朋友们安慰了。

6. He was informed by his parents.
   他的父母告诉了他。

7. I am inspired by my teacher.
   我受到老师的启发。

8. His wallet was stolen.
   他的钱包被偷了。

Whoever 无论何人

1. Whoever uses the mug must wash it.
无论谁用了杯子都要把它清洗。

2. Whoever gambles in the office will be fired.
无论谁在办公室里赌博都会被开除。

3. Whoever commits a crime will be arrested.
无论谁犯法都会被捕。

4. Whoever sings well will be chosen.
无论谁唱得好都会被选中。

5. Whoever works hard will be rewarded.
无论谁认真工作都会得到奖赏。

6. Whoever wears this hat looks good.
无论谁戴这顶帽子都好看。

7. Whoever wants to know the answer please ask me.
无论谁要知道答案都请来问我。

8. Whoever answers the phone must be polite.
无论谁接电话都要有礼貌。

Present Perfect Continuous Tense
现在完成进行时式

1. I have been playing volleyball since this morning.
   从今天早上起我一直在打排球。

2. I have been riding bicycle since this morning.
   从今天早上起我一直骑自行车。

3. I have been watching movies since this morning.
   从今天早上起我一直在看电影。

4. I have been reading since this morning.
   从今天早上起我一直在阅读。

5. He has been driving since this morning.
   从今天早上起他一直在开车。

6. He has been shopping since this morning.
   从今天早上起他一直在购物。

7. He has been complaining since this morning.
从今天早上起他一直在抱怨。

8. He has been playing games since this morning.
从今天早上起他一直在玩游戏。

Past Perfect Tense
过去完成时式

1. After I had written the letter, I went to bed.
   我写完信后，就去睡觉了。

2. After I had washed my feet, I went to bed.
   我洗了脚后，就去睡觉了。

3. After I had watered the flowers, I went to bed.
   我浇了花后，就去睡觉了。

4. After I had cleaned the toilet, I went to bed.
   我洗了厕所后，就去睡觉了。

5. After I had prayed, I went to bed.
   我祷告后，就去睡觉了。

6. After I had packed my luggage, I went to bed.
   我整理行李后，就去睡觉了。

7. After I had done my homework, I went to bed.
   我做完功课后，就去睡觉了。

8. After I had brushed my teeth , I went to bed.
   我刷牙后，就去睡觉了。

Past Perfect Continuous Tense
过去完成进行时式

1. I had been doing my homework before he came.
   在他来之前，我一直在做功课。

2. I had been watching TV before he came.
   在他来之前，我一直在看电视。

3. I had been cleaning the kitchen before he came.
   在他来之前，我一直在打扫厨房。

4. I had been sewing the clothes before he came.
   在他来之前，我一直在缝制衣服。

5. I had been talking on the phone before he came.
   在他来之前，我一直在打电话。

6. I had been studying before he came.
   在他来之前，我一直在读书。

7. I had been resting before he came.
在他来之前，我一直在休息。

8. I had been chatting before he came.
在他来之前，我一直在聊天。

If 如果 （现在式）

1. If she is angry, she will scold us.
   如果她生气了，她会骂我们。

2. If she is happy, she will laugh.
   如果她开心，她就会笑。

3. If they are sad, they will cry.
   如果他们伤心，他们会哭。

4. If the dress is expensive, she will not buy it.
   如果那件连衣裙很贵，她将不会买。

5. If the book is interesting, she will read it.
   如果这本书有趣， 她会读的。

6. If the weather is hot, she will wear a cap.
   如果天气很热，她将会戴帽子。

7. If she is busy, she will not go shopping.
   如果她忙，她将不会去购物。

8. If she is free, she will call me.
   如果她有空，她将会打电话给我。

If   如果   （过去式）

1. If he had money, he would buy a house.
   如果他有钱，他就会买一所房子。

2. If he had time, he would visit his parents.
   如果他有时间，他就会去探望他的父母。

3. If he had time, he would help me to cook.
   如果他有时间，他就会帮我做饭。

4. If he was angry, he would scold us.
   如果他生气了，他就会骂我们。

5. If he was sick, he would go to see a doctor.
   如果他生病了，他就会去看医生。

6. If he had time, he would read books.
   如果他有时间，他就会看书。

7. If they lost their way, they would call me.
   如果他们迷路了，他们就会打电话给我。

8. If they were happy, they would laugh
   loudly.
   如果他们开心，他们就会大声笑。

When   当

1. When she was reading a book, I called her.
当她在看书的时候，我打电话给她。

2. When she was walking to the library, she fell down.
当她走去图书馆的时候，她跌倒了。

3. When they were talking in the classroom, the teacher walked in.
当他们在课室里讲话的时候，老师走进来。

4. When she was washing the basin, her son fainted.
当她在洗水盆的时候，她的儿子晕倒了。

5. When they were swimming, they saw a rainbow.
当他们在游泳的时候，他们看到了一道彩虹。

6. When they were cycling, John took a photograph.
当他们在骑自行车的时候，约翰拍了一张照片。

7. When she was having her breakfast, it started to rain.
当她在吃早餐的时候，天空下起雨来。

8. When she was jogging, she injured her knee.
当她在慢跑时，她伤了膝盖。

Because　因为

1. He did not go to school because he was sick.
   他没有去上学，因为他生病了。

2. We are angry because you lied to us.
   我们生气是因为你骗了我们。

3. He cancelled the appointment because it was raining.
   他取消了约会，因为下雨了。

4. He scolded his daughter because she was naughty.
   他责骂他的女儿，因为她很淘气。

5. We did not buy the house because it was expensive.
   我们没有买那间房子，因为它很贵。

6. He did not attend the class because he was busy.
   他没有去上课，因为他很忙。

7. We were frightened because he wanted to kill us.
   我们很害怕，因为他要杀我们。

8. He left the hall because it was very noisy.
   他离开了大厅，因为里面很吵。

Since 因为

1. Since she was very naughty, her teacher punished her.
   因为她很调皮，她的老师惩罚了她。

2. Since they were tired, they went back earlier.
   因为他们很累，就早点回去了。

3. Since she is very friendly, everyone likes her.
   因为她很友善，每个人都喜欢她。

4. Since it was raining, she did not go to the park.
   由于下雨，她没有去公园。

5. Since she was sick, she went to see a doctor.
   因为她生病了，就去看医生。

6. Since they were curious, they asked a lot of questions.
   因为他们好奇，就问了很多问题。

7. Since it was a public holiday, he did not go to work.
   因为是公共假日，他没有去上班。

8. Since it was a rainy day, they stayed at home.
   因为是下雨天，他们呆在家里。

Although　虽然

1. Although we were sad, we did not cry.
   虽然我们很哀伤，我们没有哭泣。

2. Although we are poor, we are not greedy.
   虽然我们贫穷，我们不贪心。

3. Although he is an adult, he is very childish.
   虽然他是一个成年人，他很幼稚。

4. Although he is smart, he is very lazy.
   虽然他聪明，他很懒惰。

5. Although he did not understand, he nodded his head.
   虽然他不明白，但是他点点头。

6. Although he is rich, he is very thrifty.
   虽然他富有，但是他很节俭。

7. Although he is very successful, he is very humble.
   虽然他很成功，但是他很谦虚。

8. Although he was sick, he went to play football.
   虽然他生病了，但是他去踢足球。

In spite of   尽管

1. In spite of his sickness, he won the competition.
尽管他生病了，他还是赢了比赛。

2. In spite of his anger, he hugged his son.
尽管他生气了，他还是拥抱了他的儿子。

3. In spite of his carelessness, he completed the task.
尽管他很粗心，他还是完成了任务。

4. In spite of his friendliness, his colleagues dislike him.
尽管他很友善，他的同事们都不喜欢他。

5. In spite of his laziness, his boss likes him.
尽管他懒惰，他的老板还是喜欢他。

6. In spite of his poor health, he often travels.
尽管他身体不好，他还经常旅行。

7. In spite of his busy schedule, he came to help us.
    尽管他生活忙碌，他还是来帮我们。

8. In spite of his wealth, he is always unhappy.
    尽管他很富有，他总是不开心。

Whether　是否

1. I do not know whether he likes the shirt.
   我不知道他是否喜欢那件衬衫。

2. She does not know whether they are hungry.
   她不知道他们是否饿了。

3. Please tell me whether you are coming.
   请告诉我你是否会来。

4. I do not know whether he has called Jenny.
   我不知道他是否打电话给珍妮了。

5. She does not know whether John likes grapes.
   她不知道约翰是否喜欢葡萄。

6. They do not know whether these houses are expensive.
   他们不知道这些房子是否昂贵。

7. I do not know whether he is honest.
    我不知道他是否诚实。

8. I do not know whether I should tell you.
    我不知道我是否应该告诉你。

So that   以便

1. I work hard so that I can make a lot of money.
我努力工作以便能赚很多钱。

2. I exercise often so that I can be healthy.
我常做运动以便保持身体健康。

3. I sleep early so that I can wake up early.
我早睡以便能够早起。

4. I save money so that I can go for a tour.
我存钱以便能够去旅游。

5. I join the club so that I can make new friends.
我加入这俱乐部以便结交新朋友。

6. I have to make money so that I can support my family.
我必须赚钱以便养家。

7. I woke up early yesterday so that I could see the sunrise.
我昨天早起以便能看到日出。

8. We help the poor children so that they can have a better life.
我们帮助贫穷的孩子们以便他们能有更好的生活。

Who　谁

1. The girl who wore red is my friend.
   那个穿红色衣服的女孩是我的朋友。

2. The man who shouted at you is my colleague.
   那个喊你的男士是我的同事。

3. The boy who suffers from cancer is a top student.
   那位患有癌症的男孩是个优秀的学生。

4. I know the lady who sells jewellery.
   我认识那位卖珠宝的女士。

5. This is the boy who plays piano very well.
   这就是那个很会弹钢琴的男孩。

6. This is the lady who helped me.
   这就是那位帮助我的女士。

7. The man who bought the car is my classmate.
   买这辆车的那位男士是我的同学。

8. The girl who made the cake is my student.
   做蛋糕的那位女孩是我的学生。

Noun Phrases　名词短语

1. John, a chubby boy, is my younger brother.
   约翰，一个胖乎乎的男孩，是我的弟弟。

2. Mary, a salesgirl, is my best friend.
   玛丽，一个女售货员，是我最好的朋友。

3. George, an engineer, is her husband.
   乔治，一名工程师，是她的丈夫。

4. The boy, Kenny, won the first prize.
   这个男孩，肯尼，赢得了头奖。

5. Mark, a lawyer, is a very considerate man.
   马克，一名律师，是一个非常体贴的人。

6. My secretary, Susan, called the ambulance.
   我的秘书，苏珊，打电话叫了救护车。

7. John, my elder brother, taught me how
   to ski.
   约翰，我的哥哥，教了我滑雪。

8. Mary, my colleague, invited me to her
   birthday party.
   玛丽，我的同事，邀请了我去她的
   生日聚会。

Which 哪一个

1. The bag which is on the table is very expensive.
   桌子上的那个皮包很贵。

2. The necklace which I bought yesterday is very cheap.
   我昨天买的那条项链很便宜。

3. These are the shoes which are very trendy.
   这些是非常时髦的鞋子。

4. I saw the puppy which you like.
   我看见了你喜欢的那只小狗。

5. This is the raincoat which she wore yesterday.
   这是她昨天穿的雨衣。

6. I sold the house which is near the museum.
   我卖了那间靠近博物院的屋子。

7. This is the perfume which is very saleable.
这个就是很畅销的香水。

8. Those are the days which I enjoyed very much.
那些是我很享受的日子。

Whom   谁

1. The actor whom you like is coming to Singapore.
你喜欢的那位男演员要来新加坡。

2. The man whom you talked to is my boss.
那位与你谈话的男士是我的老板。

3. The girl whom he dislikes is very selfish.
他不喜欢的那个女孩很自私。

4. The child whom they adopted is very cute.
他们领养的那个小孩很可爱。

5. The students whom he taught were very playful.
他教的学生很顽皮。

6. The lady whom he met is my neighbour.
他遇到的那位女士是我的邻居。

7. The boy whom you play with is my nephew.
那个和你玩的男孩是我的侄子。

8. The man whom she argued with is a magician.
那个和她争论的男士是一名魔术师。

Whose   谁的

1. The girl whose mother is an actress bought the cake.
母亲当演员的那个女孩买了蛋糕。

2. This is the man whose wife is a lawyer.
这就是那位妻子当律师的男士。

3. This is the woman whose husband is a principal.
这就是那位丈夫当校长的女士。

4. I saw the boy whose parents are very generous.
我看到那个父母很大方的男孩。

5. The boy whose father is a police informed us.
父亲是警察的那个男孩通知我们的。

6. This is the woman whose son is a movie director.
这就是那位儿子当导演的女士。

7. The singer whose wife is a violinist wrote this song.
妻子是小提琴家的那位歌手写了这首歌。

8. The man whose daughter suffers from cancer is very depressed.
女儿患了癌症的那位男士很沮丧。

Where 哪里

1. This is the restaurant where we first met.
   这是我们第一次见面的餐馆。

2. This is the place where the accident happened.
   这是事故发生的地方。

3. I like the park where you took your wedding photos.
   我喜欢你拍婚纱照的公园。

4. The place where we went yesterday is very beautiful.
   我们昨天去的地方很漂亮。

5. The beach where they go weekly is very far.
   他们每周去的那个海滩很远。

6. I remember the place where we saw a bear.
   我记得我们看到一只熊的那个地方。

7. This is the carpark where my car was stolen.
   这就是我的车被偷的停车场。

8. This is the park where he proposed to his girlfriend.
   这就是他向女友求婚的公园。

Not only but also　不但而且

1. Not only is he very intelligent, he is also very hardworking.
他不但很聪明，而且很勤劳。

2. Not only is he very handsome, he is also very kind.
他不但很英俊，而且很善良。

3. Not only is he very childish, he is also very lazy.
他不但很幼稚，而且很懒惰。

4. Not only is he very polite, he is also very humble.
他不但很有礼貌，而且很谦虚。

5. Not only is he very healthy, he is also very cheerful.
他不但很健康，而且很开朗。

6. Not only is he very cunning , he is also very fierce.
他不但很狡猾，而且很凶。

7. Not only is he very capable, he is also very efficient.
他不但很能干，而且也很有效率。

8. Not only is he my teacher, he is also my mentor.
他不但是我的老师，而且也是我的导师。

As if   似乎

1. You look as if you have not slept for three days.
   你看起来好像三天没有睡觉了。

2. He always behaves as if he is smarter than us.
   他总是表现得好像他比我们聪明。

3. She looks as if she has never aged.
   她看起来好像没有老化。

4. He eats as if he has not eaten for a week.
   他吃得好像一个星期没有吃东西了。

5. She screamed as if someone had wanted to kill her.
   她尖叫得好像有人要杀她。

6. She cried as if she had lost a million dollar.
   她哭得好像损失了一百万元。

7. She talks to me as if she is my boss.
   她跟我说话的态度好像她是我的老板。

8. She behaves as if she is mad.
   她表现得像个疯子。

2. 集合名词

Collective Nouns

an army of soldiers
一军队兵士

an army of ants
一群蚂蚁

a band of musicians
一群音乐家

a bunch of crooks
一伙骗子

a choir of singers
一团歌手

a class of pupils
一班学生

a crowd of people
一群人

a crowd of spectators
一群观众

an album of photographs
一本相册的照片

a bouquet of flowers
一束花

a bunch of bananas
一串香蕉

a bundle of joy
一捆欢乐

a flock of chickens
一群鸡

a flock of birds
一群鸟

a herd of elephants
一群大象

3. 明瑜

Similes

1. As big as a bus
   像巴士一样大

2. As big as an elephant
   像大象一样大

3. As black as charcoal
   像火炭一样黑

4. As blind as a bat
   像蝙蝠一样瞎。

5. As brave as a lion
   像狮子一样勇敢

6. As busy as a bee
   像蜜蜂一样忙

7. As clear as a bell
   像钟声一样清晰洪亮

8. As clear as crystal
   像水晶一样明澈

9. As cold as ice
   像冰一样冷

10. As cool as a cucumber
    像黄瓜一样冷静

11. As cunning as a fox
    像狐狸一样狡猾

12. As easy as abc
    像ABC一样容易

13. As flat as a pancake
    像薄煎饼一样平

14. As free as a bird
    像鸟儿一样自由。

15. As gentle as a lamb
像羊儿一样温顺。

16. As happy as a lark
像云雀一样快乐

17. As light as a feather
像羽毛一样轻

18. As obstinate as a mule
像驴子一样固执

19. As poor as a church mouse
像教堂的老鼠一样穷

20. As proud as a peacock
像孔雀一样骄傲。

21. As pure as snow
像雪一样纯洁

22. As quick as lightning
像闪电一样快

23. As slow as a snail
像蜗牛一样慢

24. As slow as a tortoise
    像乌龟一样慢

25. As smooth as silk
    像丝绸一样滑

26. As solid as a rock
    像岩石一样坚固

27. As tall as a giraffe
    像长颈鹿一样高

28. As white as snow
    像白雪一样白

29. As wise as Solomon
    像所罗门王一样有智慧

4. 同义词

Synonyms

big	large	大
begin	start	开始
small	tiny	很小
exit	leave	离开
talk	speak	讲
clever	smart	聪明
present	gift	礼物
listen	hear	听
shut	close	关
ill	sick	生病
hard	difficult	困难

shop	store	商店
see	look	看
hat	cap	帽子
chef	cook	厨师
street	road	马路
reply	answer	回答
happy	glad	高兴
under	below	之下
fast	quick	快
evil	bad	邪恶、坏
jog	run	跑
taxi	cab	德士
rich	wealthy	富有
mistake	error	错误
shout	yell	喊
difficult	hard	困难
friend	buddy	朋友
help	assist	帮忙
neat	tidy	整齐
pair	duo	一双
walk	stroll	走

honest	candid	诚实
choose	select	选
jump	leap	跳
slim	slender	瘦、苗条

5. 反义词

Antonyms

clean	清洁	dirty	肮脏
in	进	out	出
up	上	down	下
left	左	right	右
stop	停	go	走
tall	高	short	矮
true	对	false	错
old	旧	new	新
first	第一	last	最后

win	赢	lose	输
meek	温顺	bold	胆大
work	做工	play	玩
like	喜欢	dislike	不喜欢

6. 成语

Idioms

1. a hot potato
一个热乎乎的马铃薯；棘手的问题

2. a blessing in disguise
伪装的祝福；塞翁失马；因祸得福

3. a leopard can't change his spots
一只豹不能改变它的斑点，本性难移。

4. a picture paints a thousand words
一张图片胜过千字。

5. a piece of cake
一块蛋糕；容易做的事

6. actions speak louder than words
   行动比言语更响亮; 事实胜于雄辩

7. all in the same boat
   大家同在一艘船上; 同病相怜

8. a taste of your own medicine
   尝到你自己的药; 自作自受

9. at the drop of a hat
   立刻、马上

10. back to square one
    回到原点; 问题回到原态, 并没有解决。

11. ball is in your court
    球在你的场地; 一切由你决定

12. beating around the bush
    在灌木丛周围敲打; 拐弯抹角

13. best of both worlds
    两全其美

14. blood is thicker than water
    血浓于水

15. burn the midnight oil
点燃午夜的油灯; 熬夜

16. can't judge a book by its cover
不能靠封面评断一本书; 人不可貌相

17. caught between two stools
夹在两个凳子之间; 左右为难

18. costs an arm and a leg
值一只手臂和一条腿; 价钱很贵

19. cross that bridge when you come to it
来到那座桥时才走过去; 船到桥头自然直

20. cry over spilt milk
为溢出的牛奶而哭; 作无益的后悔

21. curiosity killed the cat
好奇心害死了猫; 太过好奇会害了你

22. cut corners
走捷径; 偷工减料

23. don't put all your eggs in one basket.
不要把全部的鸡蛋放在一个篮子里; 不要
孤注一掷

24. every cloud has a silver lining
黑暗中总有一丝光明、总会有解决的办法。

25. far cry from
相去甚远; 差别很大

26. feel a bit under the weather
感觉有点在天气之下; 健康或精神不好

27. give the benefit of the doubt
先推定为无罪

28. hit the nail on the head
打中铁钉的头; 一针见血

29. hit the hay
撞干草; 睡觉去了

30. in the heat of the moment
在盛怒之下

31. it takes two to tango
探戈舞需要两个人才能跳; 一个巴掌拍不响

32. jump on the bandwagon
跳上花车; 支持流行的东西

33. keep something at bay
退避三舍

34. kill two birds with one stone
用一块石头杀两只鸟；一箭双雕

35. last straw
使人不能忍受的最后一击

36. let the cat out of the bag
让猫从袋子出来；不小心泄漏秘密

37. make a long story short
把一个长故事变短；长话短说

38. miss the boat
错过了船；错过良机

39. once in a blue moon
很久一次

40. see eye to eye
看眼对眼；看法完全一致

41. sit on the fence
坐在篱笆上；骑墙观望，犹豫不决

42. speak of the devil
     说到那魔鬼；说曹操曹操到

43. take with a grain of salt
     加一粒盐；不要完全相信

44. your guess is as good as mine
     你的猜测和我的一样好；我也不很清楚

45. add fuel to the fire
     添加汽油在火上；加油添酱

46. apple of my eye
     我眼里的苹果；我的心肝宝贝

47. cut to the chase
     单刀直入；说话直接

7. 积极的话语

Positive Words

1. I am very optimistic.
   我非常乐观。

2. I will definitely succeed.
   我一定会成功。

3. I am not afraid of failures.
   我不怕失败。

4. I want to contribute to the society.
   我要为社会做出贡献。

5. I do not like to be jealous of people.
我不喜欢妒嫉别人。

6. I am very hardworking.
我很勤劳。

7. I am confident.
我有信心。

8. I am very fortunate.
我很幸运。

9. Success comes after failure.
失败是成功之母。

10. I am very likeable.
我很讨人喜欢。

11. I love my work.
我喜欢我的工作。

12. I keep moving forward.
我一直往前走。

13. I am not afraid of hardship.
我不怕困难。

14. I love my home.
我爱我的家。

15. I love my country.
我爱我的国家。

16. I want to care for the earth.
我要爱护地球。

17. I am very happy everyday.
我每天都很开心。

18. I am very helpful.
我很喜欢帮助别人。

19. I am very brave.
我很勇敢。

20. I pray for world peace.
我祈求世界和平。

21. I believe in miracles.
我相信奇迹。

22. I treasure every day.
我珍惜每一天。

23. Everyone has their own strengths.
    每个人都有自己的长处。

24. I am a wonderful person.
    我是一个优秀的人。

25. I am very healthy.
    我很健康。

26. Life is full of hopes.
    人生充满了希望。

27. I want to travel the world.
    我要周游世界。

8. 常见的短语和句子

Common Phrases & Sentences

1. I have to go.
    我得走了。

2. I will text you.
    我将会发短信给你。

3. I will email it to you.
    我将会发电邮给你。

4. I forgot
    我忘了。

5. Be careful
    小心点

6. I lost my way.
   我迷路了。

7. I beg you.
   我求你。

8. It's my mistake.
   这是我的错误。

9. I will think about it.
   我会考虑一下。

10. I guess so.
    我猜是这样。

11. I need to consider.
    我需要考虑一下。

12. Please forgive me
    请原谅我

13. It is urgent.
    迫在眉睫

14. Please sign here
    请在这里签名。

15. It is my fault.
这是我的错。

16. We are closed today.
我们的店今天关门。

17. It is an accident.
这是一场意外。

18. Call the ambulance
叫救护车

19. Call the police
打电话报警

20. Beware of pickpockets
小心扒手

21. It's too loud.
太大声了

22. Please keep quiet
请保持安静

23. He is drunk.
他喝醉了。

24. Please lower the volume
请降低音量

25. Enjoy your day!
祝您愉快!

26. Let's dance
让我们一起跳舞

27. can't hear.
我听不到。

28. Please reply
请回答

29. What a pity
太遗憾了

30. Don't be shy
不要害羞

31. I don't understand.
我不明白

32. I feel cold.
我觉得冷。

33. It's very hot.
今天很热

34. It's freshly baked.
这是新鲜出炉的。

35. I notice it.
我注意到了。

36. Please ignore him
别理他

37. I am in trouble.
我有麻烦了。

38. I am in a hurry.
我很急。

39. I don't believe it.
我不相信。

40. I cancelled my appointment.
我取消了约会。

41. I trust you.
我信任你。

42. Please take a look
请看一下

43. It shocked me.
吓我一跳!

44. I love to shop online.
我喜欢在网上购物。

45. Please be patient
请耐心等待

46. Please wait for a moment
请稍等一下

47. I missed the bus.
我错过了巴士。

48. Please queue up
请排队

49. It's too difficult.
这太难了

50. I have a headache.
我的头疼。

51. Please silent your handphone
请静默您的手机

52. Please switch off your mobile phone
请关闭您的手机

53. I bought it online.
我在网上买了。

54. Christmas is coming soon.
圣诞节快到了。

55. It's a surprise!
这是个惊喜!

56. He is a nuisance.
他是一个滋扰。

57. It's very noisy here.
这里很吵。

58. I am serious.
我是认真的。

59. I bet with you.
我跟你打赌。

60. Let me make a guess
    让我猜猜

61. It's a scam.
    这是一个骗局。

62. He sprained his ankle.
    他扭伤了他的脚踝。

63. Close your eyes
    闭上你的眼睛

64. I doubt It.
    我对此表示怀疑。

65. I forgot my password.
    我忘了我的密码。

66. I forgot my user ID.
    我忘了我的用户名。

67. I want to buy a phone card.
    我要买一张电话卡。

68. I missed my flight.
    我错过了班机。

69. I need a break.
我需要休息。

70. Please switch off the air conditioner
请关闭空调。

71. Please switch on the light
请开灯

72. Please answer the phone
请接电话

73. Please call me tomorrow
明天请打电话给我

74. She hanged up the phone.
她挂了电话。

75. He picked up the call.
他接了电话。

76. Please fasten your seat belt.
请绑安全带

77. He is drunk.
他喝醉了。

78. He is talking nonsense.
他在说废话。

79. Please bring a jacket
请带一件夹克

80. I invited him to the party.
我邀请他参加聚会。

81. He took a photograph.
他拍了一张照片。

82. She is pregnant.
她怀孕了。

83. It's a misunderstanding.
这是一个误会。

84. I booked a taxi.
我订了一辆出租车。

85. I have changed my mind.
我改变主意了。

86. I am just curious.
我只是好奇。

87. I have made up my mind.
我已经决定了。

88. I am stressed.
我的压力很大。

89. I have resigned.
我已经辞职。

90. He is a con man.
他是一个骗子。

91. Please bring your passport
请携带您的护照

92. John married Jenny.
约翰和珍妮结婚。

93. The road is very slippery.
这条路很滑。

94. It's a miracle.
这是一个奇迹。

9. 常见的问题

Common Questions

1. Have you made a reservation?
   您预订了吗？

2. Did you make an appointment?
   你预约了吗？

3. Do you have wifi?
   你有无线网络吗？

4. What is your phone number?
   你的电话号码几号？

5. What is the password?
   密码是什么？

6. **What's the matter?**
   怎么了?

7. **Will you be free tomorrow?**
   你明天有空吗?

8. **Are you sick?**
   你生病了吗?

9. **May I use your phone?**
   我可以用你的电话吗?

10. **Shall we take a picture?**
    我们拍张照片好吗?

11. **Shall we go?**
    我们该走了吗?

12. **How is your day?**
    你今天过得怎么样?

13. **How's the weather?**
    天气怎么样?

14. **Could you help me?**
    你可以帮我吗 ?

15. Would you help me?
你能帮我吗?

16. Is it possible?
是否可以?

17. How big is the table?
桌子有多大?

18. Are you hungry?
你饿了吗 ?

19. Are you tired?
你累吗?

20. When is your wedding anniversary?
你们的结婚纪念日是几时?

21. When are you coming?
你什么时候要来?

22. Why are you crying?
为什么你在哭?

23. What time is your flight?
你的航班是什么时候?

24. Did you call me?
    你打电话给我吗?

25. Do you agree?
    你同意吗?

26. Do you miss me?
    你想念我吗?

27. Who is your boss?
    谁是你的老板?

28. Where do you park your car?
    你把车停泊在哪里?

29. Do you like chocolates?
    你喜欢吃巧克力吗?

30. What is your email address?
    你的电邮地址是什么?

31. What is your ambition?
    你的志向是什么?

32. May I speak with Jenny?
    我可以和珍妮谈谈吗?

33. Is Mr Li in?
李先生在吗?

34. May I borrow your pen?
我可以借用你的钢笔吗?

35. Did you receive my message?
你有没有收到我的讯息?

36. Did you lock the door?
你有没有锁门?

37. Have you decided?
你决定了吗?

38. Have you informed her?
你通知她了吗?

39. Where is the carpark?
停车场在哪里?

40. Are you a member?
您是会员吗?

41. How much is the membership fee?
会员费是多少?

10. 词汇

Vocabulary

Bank 银行

cheque	支票
cash	现金
deposit	存款
withdraw	支出
interest	利息
foreign exchange	外汇
bank Account	银行账户
credit Card	信用卡
service	服务

Restaurant 餐馆

chef	厨师
waiter	男侍应生
waitress	女侍应生
bill	账单
delicious	美味
sauce	酱汁
chilli	辣椒
pepper	胡椒粉
order	点菜
menu	菜单
reasonable	合理
price	价钱
utensils	餐具
saucer	小碟子
tea spoon	茶匙
spoon	汤匙
chopsticks	筷子
warm water	温水
set meal	套餐

Food 食物

fried chicken	炸鸡
beef steak	牛排
chicken chop	鸡排
lamb chop	羊排
fried noodle	炒面
noodle soup	汤面
fish fillet	鱼片
salad	沙拉
appetiser	开胃菜
dessert	甜品
seafood	海鲜
shrimp	虾
fried vegetable	炒菜
mushroom soup	蘑菇汤
roast duck	烧鸭
pizza	意大利薄饼
spring roll	春卷
curry fish head	咖喱鱼头
dumplings	水饺

Supermarket 超级市场

vegetable	蔬菜
fruits	水果
fresh	新鲜
cashier	收银员
trolly	手推车
snacks	零食
mineral water	矿泉水
confectionery	糕饼
frozen food	冷冻食品

Clinic 诊所

injection	打针
fever	发烧
flu	流感
dizzy	头晕
stomachache	肚子痛
headache	头痛
blood pressure	血压
doctor	医生
nurse	护士

Food Court 食阁

stall	摊位
prawn noodle	虾面
porridge	粥
chicken rice	鸡饭
fish soup	鱼汤
fish ball	鱼丸
coffee	咖啡
tea	茶
queue up	排队

Hospital 医院

emergency	紧急事件
identity card	身份证
blood test	验血
urine test	验尿
specialist	专科医生
ward	病房
blood pressure	血压
operating room	手术室
surgery	手术
medical check up	身体检查
X ray	X 光
scan	扫描
diagnosis	诊断
drug	药
mask	口罩
stethoscope	听诊器
blood donation	捐血
wheelchair	轮椅
blood transfusion	输血

Sicknesses 疾病

cancer	癌症
pneumonia	肺炎
stroke	中风
heart disease	心脏病
vomit	呕吐
diarrhoea	腹泻
hypertension	高血压
anaemia	贫血
diabetes	糖尿病

Human Organs 人体器官

kidney	肾脏
liver	肝脏
lung	肺
heart	心
bone	骨骼
intestine	肠
brain	头脑
pancreas	胰脏
blood vessel	血管

Airport 机场

passport	护照
visa	签证
check in	登机手续
air steward	男空服人员
air stewardess	女空服人员
departure hall	出境厅
arrival hall	抵境厅
luggage	行李
duty free shop	免税店

Christmas 圣诞节

Christmas tree	圣诞树
cake	蛋糕
gift	礼物
Santa Claus	圣诞老人
decorate	布置
joy	喜乐
hope	希望
peace	平安
party	派对
turkey	火鸡
candle	蜡烛
celebrate	庆祝
church	教堂
carols	圣歌
holiday	假期
Christmas eve	平安夜
Jesus	耶稣
pray	祈祷
blessing	祝福

Car Accident 车祸

ambulance	救护车
police car	警车
drunk driver	醉酒司机
death	死亡
injured	受伤
paramedics	医护人员
bleed	流血
collide	相撞
speed	速度
passerby	过路人
reporter	记者
on the spot	当场
victim	受害者
serious	严重
eyewitness	目击者
reckless	鲁莽
passenger	乘客
pedestrian	行人
deceased	死者

Character 性格

proud	骄傲
humble	谦虚
boastful	自夸
patient	有耐性
impatient	没耐性
bossy	专横的
submissive	服从的
cheerful	开朗
optimistic	乐观
pessimistic	悲观
brave	勇敢
timid	胆小
ambitious	雄心勃勃
unambitious	胸无大志
stubborn	固执
gentle	温柔
generous	慷慨
stingy	吝啬
stern	严肃

Dental Clinic 牙科诊所

dentist	牙医
denture	假牙
check	检查
decayed tooth	蛀牙
extract a tooth	拔牙
fill a tooth	补牙
nervous	紧张不安
painful	很痛
anaesthetic	麻醉剂

Concert 音乐会

harp	竖琴
cello	大提琴
violin	小提琴
piano	钢琴
conductor	指挥
pianist	钢琴师
violinist	小提琴家
orchestra	交响乐团
flute	长笛
solo	独奏
duet	二重奏
perform	表演
audience	观众
applause	鼓掌
ticket	门票
melodious	悠扬
soprano	女高音
tenor	男高音
renowned	闻名

Weather 天气

windy	有风
rain	雨
snow	雪
sunny	有阳光的
fine	晴朗
storm	暴风雨
thunder storm	雷雨
tornado	龙卷风
foggy	有雾

Marriage 婚姻

wedding gown	婚纱
register	注册
best men	伴郎
bridesmaid	伴娘
prepare	准备
wedding banquet	婚宴
guests	宾客
blissful	幸福
makeup	化妆

11. 形容词比较和最高级形容词

Comparative and Superative of adjectives

angry	angrier	angriest
生气	更生气	最生气

big	bigger	biggest
大	更大	最大

cheerful	more cheerful	most cheerful
开朗	更开朗	最开朗

cute	cuter	cutest
可爱	更可爱	最可爱

cold	colder	coldest
冷	更冷	最冷

early	earlier	earliest
早	更早	最早

fat	fatter	fattest
胖	更胖	最胖

happy	happier	happiest
开心	更开心	最开心

hot	hotter	hottest
热	更热	最热

kind	kinder	kindest
善良	更善良	最善良

late	later	latest
迟	更迟	最迟

loud	louder	loudest
大声	更大声	最大声

long	longer	longest
长	更长	最长

narrow	narrower	narrowest
窄	更窄	最窄

playful	more playful	most playful
调皮	更调皮	最调皮

quick	quicker	quickest
快	更快	最快

quiet	quieter	quietest
静	更静	最静

| short | shorter | shortest |
| 短 | 更短 | 最短 |

| slow | slower | slowest |
| 慢 | 更慢 | 最慢 |

| strong | stronger | strongest |
| 强壮 | 更强壮 | 最强壮 |

| sweet | sweeter | sweetest |
| 甜 | 更甜 | 最甜 |

| careful | more careful | most careful |
| 小心 | 更小心 | 最小心 |

| careless | more careless | most careless |
| 粗心 | 更粗心. | 最粗心 |

important	more important	most important
重要	更重要	最重要

intelligent	more intelligent	most intelligent
聪明	更聪明	最聪明

tall	taller	tallest
高	更高	最高

thin	thinner	thinnest
瘦	更瘦	最瘦

warm	warmer	warmest
温暖	更温暖	最温暖

end

Thank you for your support!
Please visit us @ englishmadesupereasy.com

Printed in the United States
By Bookmasters